Coffee Shop God

Therese Bartholomew

Coffee Shop God

Therese Bartholomew

A division of Central Piedmont Community College

Some names have been changed to protect identities both person and
company. *Coffee Shop God* title essay was previously published in
Emrys Journal, Volume 23, Spring 2006.

Published by
CPCC Press
PO Box 35009
Charlotte, NC 28235
www.cpcc.edu Keyword: Press
cpccpress@cpcc.edu

Cover Design by Susan Alford
Author and Film photographs courtesy of LunahZon Photography.
www.lunahzon.com

ISBN: 978-1-59494-038-5
Published and Printed in the United States of America

CPCC Press is a division of Central Piedmont Community College.

DEDICATION

For my brother Steve, who is never too far away

I spend days looking back, knocking on doors and peering through the windows of childhood, wandering through the hallways of houses long past...

I walk in to see my child-self sitting Indian style on the purple shag carpet. The chalkboard is leaning against the dresser. My hands are covered in dry, dusty chalk. My walls are covered in Shaun Cassidy images. I don't know how many posters there are, but they look like wallpaper disconnected at the Scotch-taped edges.

You are my best friend sitting in front of the chalkboard. Today, you are my student eagerly awaiting an assignment. Your hair is shiny blond-brown parted too far to one side. Your striped collared shirt makes you look like a little man.

I walk out alone, my bare feet sweeping across the carpet like it is grass, and when I turn around the chalkboard is clean wetness, and you're no longer there.

GRIEF

Joe, Therese & Steve with
friends, 1972

Therese & Doug, 2003

Therese & Steve, 2000

Middle of the Night

The phone rings, but I do not budge. I can't decipher in distant sleep — reality, dream, reality, dream. Doug gets up and stumbles heavy across the bedroom to answer it.

I fight opening my eyes even though the overhead shows light on the backs of my drawn lids. His voice rubs hollow and calm against a growing knot in my stomach.

"Yes. Are you sure?"

I sit up, eyes squinted, and watch Doug nod his head up and down, as if the caller can see him do this. His glassed eyes stare straight down at me, and I know something is wrong. I crawl to the end of the bed and kneel. My mind races through everyone's whereabouts — my kids,

Doug's kids, my brothers, my parents. It's Joe, I think. Life finally caught up to him. Luck ran out. He's only been out of prison a year. God, my poor parents. "What? What is it?"

The phone drags across the floor behind Doug, and he walks slow motion toward the bed. "No, no, I'll call them." He hangs up and inhales heavily through his nose. This is what he does when he's nervous. "Steve's been shot." A heavy breathed sigh — in and out before the words come. "He's dead."

My upright kneel collapses and denial takes hold. "He's at a sales meeting in Greenville. I talked to him last night. He'll be back tomorrow. There's a mistake. Who was that?" My voice cracks and so do I. "This isn't real." I hear my own shaking voice bounce around inside the blackness of the night and my mind. A whimper of sound moves up again. "This isn't real."

Doug sees I'm begging for the dream now. He lowers his face in front of me, and I know this is my life tonight, and I'd like to trade it in for someone else's and I'd like to go back to sleep and wake up tomorrow and call my brother and live again because I surely will not survive.

"Who was that?"

Doug moves in closer and grabs my shoulders.

I scoot back. "It's a mistake."

"Therese, it was Clay. Steve still had his old address on his driver's license, so they sent someone there."

"He must have misunderstood something. This doesn't make sense."

Clay lives in the house Steve used to live in. They were neighbors. Friends.

I stand up to feel something real. To feel the carpet on my feet and my new husband near me in the middle of this cold February night. But I fall.

Not really a fall, more of a slow slouch downward to the floor, and Doug braces me, but I am growing heavier and the room is sucking me down and the earth is pulling me in. My little brother is alone somewhere, and I need to be there. I need us to be kids again, snuggled in the top bunk. I need to spend summer hours crouched in our gravel driveway, feeling my palms brush and push the rocks to the side, creating cities and towns and neighborhoods for our Matchbox cars.

Doug melts down with me because he has no choice. Only a few months back I was his choice. We pushed our wedding up to November because we were practically living together anyway. Originally, we were supposed to get married ten days from now. Now, the two of us sit, the day before Valentine's, our backs pressed firm against the metal bed frame. His legs straight out and mine curled in, in their own little hug against my chest.

"What happened?"

Doug gives what he knows, and then the two of us sit in silence staring straight ahead into the open closet.

A small mound of shoes, mixed and mingled, spills from it, and I remember how when Steve and I were kids we'd hide in my closet during thunderstorms. We'd push the clothes to one side and sit right on top of the shoes, the skates, and the crap. Together, squished in breathy blackness in that tiny space, we'd swap whispers until I declared the storm had passed.

I stare at the shoes and realize I will be the one to

call Steve's children, who live with their mom in Charleston. I will be the one to call my children, spending the night with their father, my ex-husband. I will be the one that my parents will etch forever in their memories as death's messenger. Tears hit and my body shakes hard against the bed frame, and I think maybe I'll shove my clothes to the side and climb into the closet and pray for this storm to pass.

But there is a job to be done. I am the planner, the middle child, the handler. The one who interpreted Steve's toddler grunts — for a cookie or a sandwich or a drink. I took care of him. Not because my parents wouldn't have. Not because I had to, but because that's the way it was. That was the unspoken agreement when I was two and a half and Steve was born. The way it was until my parents talked to a counselor who advised them that when Steve started preschool he should attend one that was all his. One where I couldn't take care of him, one where he could learn to fend for himself. Although I adamantly disagreed with this decision, my foot stomping didn't matter, and Steve was on his own — for a while.

"We have to call my parents and the kids. My parents." I start to cry again but pull myself together and wipe the wet from under my nose. "We should go over there."

"I'm going to call Susan," Doug says and gets up for the phone.

I know he's in over his head, but so am I. He calls his sister, and I hear the word again. *Shot.*

Doug scoops me from the floor and puts my arms one at a time into the sleeves of my black wool coat. I feel him shake in quiet tears behind me. "Let's go wait in the living room."

"We should call Father Greg," I say, walking down the hall.

My parents have always loved Father Greg, and I can't go to their house empty-handed. But the priest doesn't answer the phone, so we decide to drive by the church on the way.

When Susan comes in, I'm sitting on the couch near the door. She doesn't say a word but wraps herself around me like a big sister.

It's almost two in the morning and the slow blinks of my eyes are the only thing that grounds me.

"Let's go," she whispers and doesn't fully unwrap from me. We both know that if she does I may stop moving through this night. I may hand it over to her or to Doug or to someone else in what's left of my family.

I know the air is cold because it is February and a hot little breath escapes me when I hit the outside.

Slow blinks take it in — the light hanging over our stoop, the night trees, the sky. We walk to her SUV and Susan talks to Doug and he talks back and I scoot into the back seat with Susan, and the voices are lost and scattered around the inside of the car. We drive and lights sneak in between blinks. The seat is cool leather, and I am grateful that I can feel it.

"I need to call Cil."

I grab my cell phone from my coat pocket, and I call while Susan keeps me tucked under her arm. It rings, and

I know that feeling. Good news waits for morning light. I picture Steve's ex-wife fighting not to answer the call. Fighting to fall back to sleep. Fighting reality. She answers. I tell her and she screams and I want to scream, but I don't. I tell her to be strong for the kids and then I hear the kids in the background. I hear them asking her what's wrong and I have to hang up because I have just destroyed their teenage world.

We pull down the long driveway to the rectory. Doug pounds on the door while Susan and I sit silent in the back seat of her car. She has no clue what to say and that doesn't matter because her leg is warm against mine.

I blink and a light inside the rectory comes on. Doug looks toward it, but then moves off the porch toward the flashing blue lights that have pulled in behind us and beside us.

The priest looks out the lit window.

The police approach Doug and the side of our car, and I hear them talking. Something about an intruder. The police are calm and polite and it's as if there is some secret communication that occurs after a murder because the police seem to know why we're here, and one mouths *I'm sorry* toward me sitting inside the car. And he does look sorry.

Father Greg comes out and one of the officers walks over to talk with him for a minute and it's clear he now understands what is happening. Father waves toward Doug and turns to go into his house and I blink a prayer that he'll come back, so I don't have to go to my parents' house alone.

He does come back out with a coat on and gets in his car and follows us up the driveway and toward my parents' house.

A few blocks from the house, I call my ex-husband to tell him what has happened and to ask him to bring the kids to my parents'. He cries out because he was one of my brother's best friends. I know the next time I see my teenage kids, they will be broken. Missing the uncle who was more a father to them. I swallow that thought hard as we pull in behind my dad's Volvo. We get out just as Father

Greg pulls in. He walks up and hugs me but doesn't say a word. We walk together across the dark yard until the motion light hits us all square at the steps.

The four of us stand huddled on my parents' cluttered porch. Steve and I spent hours on this porch, side by side in the wooden swing – the metal chains grinding rhythmically as we swung back and forth and back and forth, our legs in unison. When we finally got tired, we'd jump, hand in hand, to our feet. The swing would bounce back hard against the chains, and we'd run across the porch before Mom could appear at the screen door with one of her *don't do thats*.

Doug knocks, and my dad's jarred silhouette appears just inside the door, and I know the feeling in his gut. I know that until right now my parents slept unsuspecting in a warm bed with a miniature poodle snuggled between them like a baby. The locks click. The door opens just as my mother stumbles from the darkness of the hall. Barely awake, they see us standing in a pack at the door. Me, like a little girl, still in pajamas.

I take in a cold breath. "Steve was shot. He's dead." No tears, no need to sweeten the tragic thing that has four people gathered on their front porch in the middle of the night. Dad braces himself on the door. We all scoot inside.

Father Greg steps forward to take some burden from me. He embraces my mother like she was his own. She doesn't cry but leans on the strength of this priest who isn't much older than her dead son.

We all sit scattered in the living room, my parents on the couch and me on the floor in front of them.

"What happened?" Dad asks. Miss Kitty is a ball of black fluff in his lap. "We just talked to him today. He was only going to be in Greenville for a night."

I am hesitant to tell the truth. Maybe it's not true. Maybe there was a mistake. There are mistakes. "He had gone to happy hour at a club across the street from his hotel. There was some kind of altercation with another patron, something about a girl who worked there. Evidently, Steve and the other guy were asked to leave but continued to argue in the parking lot. The guy pulled a gun and shot him in the chest." The words don't feel real when I say them. "It was a strip club," I say. This is the real blow.

I watch my dad unfold before me. He looks like someone punched him in the stomach. Like he won't recover. His gray-black hair sprouts around his head the way I remember it looking in early morning. He looks older, weaker, like *he* suddenly needs *me*. I have the urge to hug him, but that has never been our relationship. His hugs are awkward and intentional. This is just part of my dad — like a mustache or eyeglasses. He has never once *said* he loves me. But it isn't just me; he doesn't say it to anyone. "Me too," he'd always say when my mom said I love you. "Me too," and that was it.

I blink and take in my mother, who sits beside him more matter of fact — not letting the news sink into her the way he already has. Her long silver hair drapes her breasts and covers the top of her nightgown. She reminds me of a larger version of my grandmother. The way my grandmother would take her hair down at night and pull it back into a tight bun during the day. "Have you called Joe?" my mother asks.

"Not yet," Doug jumps in. "We'll go pick him up. You'll be okay?" he asks, looking down at me sitting, legs crossed, coat still on. Susan comes from somewhere behind me, and the two of them leave to get my older brother.

When the door closes behind them, I am left with a priest and my parents. My dad says we should pray the rosary, so the three of us follow him to the dining room. My dad sits at the head of the table and pulls a worn rosary from his pocket. My mom and Father Greg sit on either side of him.

"Why was he at a strip club?" Dad asks, fingering those beads.

I kneel on the worn area rug between the living and dining room. "I guess because men like boobs." I hear the harshness of my words, but I know the truth in this. The three of them sit in that semicircle of judgment around the dining room table looking down on me.

The hardwood floor beneath the rug presses strong against my knees, and I stay upright repeating Hail Marys after my father.

The front door slams and Joe rounds the corner followed by Susan and Doug. Still kneeling, I look up at my older brother. His bloody knuckles hang near my face.

"Hit the refrigerator," he says and shakes his hand.

I only nod at that.

Joe's face is blotchy red. He's wearing a T-shirt with cutoff sleeves. No coat. This is his everyday attire. Weddings, baptisms, funerals — it doesn't matter. He's sleeveless with thinning strings of black and gray hair right past his shoulders, and that damn FTW (fuck the world) prison tattoo on display like art.

I scan the room but stop at my dad. The guilty disappointment on his face is undeniable as he looks at his oldest son. Dad knows, like all of us, that Joe is the son who should be dead — the middle-of-the-night phone call son. Joe is the one who took our family on his ride of addiction for more than twenty years, the one who has served time in almost every prison in North Carolina. It was Joe who dealt drugs through our mail slot while my parents watched *Fantasy Island* on TV. He was the one who had been shot in the chest with a .38-caliber handgun and *survived*, and now, he is the one, at almost thirty-nine, who claims his last prison visit helped him find God.

I sit back on my heels, hands on my knees, staring at my family. I want my little brother back.

I wonder if they, like me, are running down a list of people they'd rather see dead.

I blink slow and heavy and wonder if I'm on their lists.

Steve & his son, Matt
Lake Jocassee

Steve & Jessica on her
second birthday

Therese & Steve, 2001

He Looks Good

The small brick building sits across from the cemetery where he'll be buried. Where my mom's parents are buried. Where my parents already own their plots. Snow rarely covers the ground in Charlotte, but since noon it's been falling pretty steadily, and I'm surprised by the turnout. "People will be afraid to drive," I said on the way over. But the place is packed, and I know my brother is worth the drive.

His body lies at the front of the room, surrounded by pictures of him — with his kids, with my kids, with all of our friends and our family.

One of our friends built two large easels to display Steve's nature photography in the back of the room. Steve would spend hours planning camping trips and then wake before dawn to capture the perfect sunrise over a North Carolina mountain. He'd set up his camera at a stream and wait for the foaming water to lift an orange leaf in just the right way.

At precisely seven, the deacon from my parents' church asks everyone to move on into the room to say a decade of the rosary. I take a seat beside my husband in the front row. I smooth the black dress I just purchased today.

"We're closing because of the weather," the sales-girl had said through the metal gate.

"I need a dress," I said, and tears started down my pale face. "Please, just let me buy a dress. It's for my brother's funeral."

Her outlined eyes softened. "I'm sorry." She stooped down and pulled on the bottom of the gate. "You're a four or a six right?" The gate rolled up like a garage door and slammed when it reached the top. "Black dress?"

"Yes," I said, and she put her arm around me.

She took me to a dressing room, left, and came back a few minutes later with three different black dresses. I undressed in front of the mirror. My body looked frail and colorless in the harsh lights. It looked as if it no longer belonged to me. I bought the first dress I tried on and drove home in the snow.

When Deacon Robert finishes no one knows quite what to do, so I stand. "If you'd like to come forward and pay your respects that would be fine." My husband grabs my hand and moves with me to the front of the room. We stand a few feet from Steve, hosting this last party. I don't want to hug or shake hands or be cordial or polite. I want to climb into one of Steve's nature photos and forget this is my world. Maybe a mountain scene or maybe the time-lapsed beach sunrise.

The funeral director, who's as stiff as my brother, paces the room in his gray pinstriped suit as people file in to see Steve one last time. I feel like we're on his clock, and I'm taking my time.

My parents are in the foyer talking, and Joe won't budge from the front door. He won't get too near death. I blame this on an old family friend. When my aunt died, Joe was three, and some "helpful" adult tried to make sense of death by likening it to a sleep you never wake from. Well meaning, but creepy. From then on, not only did Joe fear dying but sleeping as well. He refused to sleep with the lights out. As he got older, when we'd pass cemeteries he'd take a deep breath and cover his nose and mouth just in case death was catching. No recovering from that.

"He looks good," people say as they pass Steve. "Natural. Peaceful."

What the fuck? I think. There's nothing natural or peaceful about this day, but I smile anyway. "I'll be right back." I squeeze Doug's hand and walk over to the casket my dad and I picked out yesterday.

The two of us perused the aisles together in the back of this funeral home. There were tasteful caskets with satin bedding for the comfort of the dead. And not so tasteful prom tuxedo-colored ones with words circling the heads. We chose a wheat-colored wood for Steve.

For a second, I ponder climbing in with Steve —
snuggling him one last time before his life is closed.

The detective said he died instantly. "He never saw
it coming," he said, sitting at my mom's dining room table
the day after the murder.

Steve is in the suit he and I picked out together not
even a year ago when he took me to the prom at the school
where I teach. I look over my shoulder at the teenagers, my
brother's and mine. They sit separate and broken right in
front. The girls embrace between tears. The boys sit side
by side in new suits on a plush red Victorian couch.

Last night I gathered the four of them in the den
downstairs. I told them how much I loved them, and how
much Steve would always love them. That they would
survive because they were strong. That it was okay to be
angry with God and the world and anyone they needed
to be angry with. Even though I don't fully believe any of
us will survive, I am the mom, and I knew this was what I
should say.

Only two months ago we had all gone to the mountains together for Christmas. The girls heard a noise in the

middle of the night that sent them both running across the cabin to Steve's room, where they slept until morning.

He had been the first man to hold my daughter, Jessica. When I came home pregnant in high school he said, "I'll help you." We swung back and forth on the front porch swing. "You don't need him," he said when my boy-friend stopped returning my calls. And from then on it was the big pregnant girl and a small entourage of ninth-grade boys walking around our neighborhood.

Now, Jessica sits staring at a wheat-colored casket full of her world, and I wonder who she'll be without him.

I hate that my stepchildren will never know their new uncle. A missed opportunity for all four of them. Little and needy and all full of gaps Steve would have tried to fill. Not now.

People circle past the kids and the casket with un-comfortable smiles and whispers. "That's his son, daugh-ter, niece, nephew. That's his ex-wife." Whoever. "He looks good," they all say and keep on walking.

Limpy (a.k.a Dimpers)

Steve & Trea
Backpacking trip, 2002

Therese, Steve & friend, Laurel
Grandma's front porch, 1977

Menagerie

We pull up to my brother's house two days after the funeral. The porch light is on in the middle of the day. The yellow paint we retouched just last summer greets us like any old day's sunshine. Doug stops the Expedition right in front.

"Well, we can't leave him here," I say to the kids. "What if the heat goes out? He'll freeze. It shouldn't take long with all of us here. Trea, grab the travel cage."

Getting out of the car, I have a strong feeling the bird is already contemplating which one of us he'll bite first. African Greys are known for being as smart as a two-year-old child with about the same propensity for biting. Steve adopted him almost two years ago when his old roommate decided a bird was too demanding. None of us have ever been able to handle him. Limpy (named because of the nubby right foot he's had since birth) has always been a one-man bird, and now the one man is dead.

Trea pops the back hatch, and pulls out the cage. He lumbers behind us, six-foot-two and silent about entering his uncle's house. We walk up the stairs, and I think about how many times Steve and I sat out on this porch — him playing guitar and me slipping back and forth in the black wrought-iron glider. It isn't just this house, but the neighborhood, that holds so many memories.

My mom grew up next door, where my grandmother lived until she moved in with my parents in the early nineties. As kids, Steve and I spent hours in that yard and the alley next to it. The alley was lined with blackberry bushes, which we regularly picked clean until one summer when a black snake chased Steve up one of the iron porch columns and me into the house. I stood right inside the screen door giving orders while he clung to the black bars. "Wait a few minutes, until we know he's gone," I said panting and holding a plastic cup full of the snake's berries.

"Now!" I yelled, and Steve climbed down and ran across the wood porch to me holding the screen door open. The door slammed, and we stood with our faces pressed against the screen looking for the snake.

Doug puts his hand in the small of my back as I unlock the door and step inside. One after the other we fill the living room. The house feels hollow.

Doug has already taken the two dogs, Dale and Ellie, to our place so they can go back to Charleston in a few days with Matt and Tami, Steve's teenage kids. Even though their mother is by no means an animal lover, the kids' plea for the dogs took less than a minute. The three cats — Lucy, Shithead (pronounced She-theed), and Junior — have been taken in by various friends.

Tami walks past me and toward the kitchen, where yesterday I saw a half-empty bottle of cabernet on the counter right beside a pizza pan and cutter and crumbs from a few days back. I'd left it all in its place, thinking maybe if I left it, Steve would come back to clean up.

The massive wooden and wire cage sits in the corner of the dining room right next to a window. Limpy's on his perch, puffed in gray and white feathers with that red bunch peeking out the back like some old lady's slip. The bright red fan unfolds when he stretches and fluffs his gray coat.

"Limpy," I whisper and walk in toward the cage. "What is it, Limpy? We're going for a ride, Dimpers." I shake my head, thinking how strange and funny that Steve gave the bird a pet name. "You miss him, don't you, Dimpers?" I wrap my fingers loosely around the front of the cage while he watches me.

Limpy's repertoire has become quite extensive, and the bulk of it is an exact mimic of Steve's voice. If you didn't know better, you would assume Steve was the one saying *here Ellie* followed by clicking noises, or *com'ere girl* or *feel my wing, boy*, which he'd say and drag out the *boy* part so he'd sound just like Steve's favorite cartoon charac-ter, Foghorn Leghorn.

More than the other animals, giving away this one will be like giving away a piece of my brother, and I have no idea where to place him. The bird has to be cared for in a different way, and until I can figure out the least traumatic plan possible, I have decided to temporarily take him on. The biggest problem, of course, will be in transferring him from one cage to another and then from one house to another. Not only am I concerned about the basics, like moving and feeding him without losing a digit, but I wonder if he will ever talk again, or if he'll ever bond with a new owner.

Doug puts his hand on my shoulder, and we stand contemplating Limpy's move.

"Okay, who's going to grab him?" I say, staring into the cage and praying for a volunteer to step up.

"You're crazy," Matt says, wandering in behind Trea, who has the travel cage. "There is no way I'm putting my hand near that bird."

Trea puts the travel cage down beside me. My daughter, Jessica, and Tami come in and move toward the big cage. We are all gathered as if we are onlookers at the zoo. Matt backs away and plops down at the dining room table right behind us.

"Why not just open the cage and let him get out?" Jessica says with sixteen-year-old authority. She drags the little cage around to the front door of the big one. "What if we set this cage here, open the door, and then wait? I mean, where else is he going to go?" Jess grabs a peanut from Limpy's treat basket and tosses it into the small cage in an effort to coax him.

The bird's nubby feet hold to the wire door of his cage. "All right, it's worth a shot," I chime in, "and, if he gets out one of us can grab him with a towel or something."

"Who's gonna grab him?" Matt says.

"I don't know." I open the cage door slowly, and everyone backs away. As the door opens, step by step, Limpy moves sideways toward the corner of his cage.

We decide he'll be more apt to come out if we move into the adjoining living room. So, with the cage fully open, we step out to wait.

It doesn't take long for him to fly out and over the travel cage. He hobbles across the floor and through the

French doors toward us.

"Where's the towel?" I say, taking charge of the situation. Matt tosses it to me, and I waddle behind the bird with the towel outstretched, waiting for the perfect moment. I go in a few times, but Limpy picks up the pace and moves quickly across the hardwood floor. I stand back up in defeat. "There's no way. I'm not going to catch this bird."

Jess steps in. "I'll do it. Give me the towel." I hand her the towel and she begins her hunt, the towel outstretched and her tennis shoes squeaking as she does this crazy dance with the disabled bird. She gets right down on him before he speeds up, and all I can think is how much my brother must be laughing as our inept group tries to wrangle his gimp-legged bird. Jess and Limpy are circling the floor between the living and dining rooms.

With her legs spread and the towel right behind him, Jess swoops in suddenly. "Damn it," Limpy says and picks up his pace. We all glance around the room with did-he-just-say-that looks on our faces. Laughter breaks out, but Jess doesn't lose focus, and this time Limpy's little legs can't outrun the worn towel. Jess scoops him up and moves quickly toward the travel cage. She shoves him in, and I run over and shut the cage door. Doug covers the cage with a blanket because I'm afraid this nutty bird will get sick in the February air. I'm afraid he won't adjust, or he'll never talk again, or he'll just die from his little birdie grief.

When we get home, we put the small cage on top of the TV armoire in the living room. This is the busiest part of the house, the place where he'll get plenty of attention. Doug slowly removes the blanket from the cage. Limpy is pacing back and forth with fluffed feathers. *Wearing your puffy coat?* Steve used to inquire when Limpy did this, and I remember the bird acts this way when he gets nervous.

It's getting late, and everyone scatters to corners of the house while I stand contemplating the fate of the bird. I lean forward toward the cage. "It's okay, Dimpers," I whisper. Limpy climbs up to the front of the cage and looks down at me. I cautiously stroke his feet, thinking if he comes in for a bite, I'll have time to move my fingers. He bows his head as if to say *pet me*, but I don't. I've seen this ploy before. Steve would have a guest, someone new to the bird, and before the warning would make it out, Limpy would lure the newcomer to the cage with a lowered head. It's pretty amazing how fast the bird can lift his head once a finger moves in. For just this reason, I've never been brave enough to stick a finger anywhere near him until now.

I stand on my tiptoes to check his food bowl. I press a finger to the metal tip of the water bottle, and water drips slowly out. "I'm going to bed, Limpy." I walk across the room and turn off the overhead light. "Good night, Dimpers," I say and head down the hall.

The first two days, the bird doesn't eat more than the occasional peanut I hand through the wires of his cage. For the most part, he paces back and forth and back and forth like a crooked old man. I talk to him every time I walk through the living room, and while I'm cooking dinner, and I say goodbye when I leave the house. Sometimes I just sit on the couch and converse with him as if he were an old friend. Occasionally, he stops pacing long enough to stare me down, as if to say *how long will this visit last?* Even if he asks, I can't answer this question.

While the kids are at school, I wander the lonely house as if it is my own little cage. The bird and I seem to have an unspoken agreement with everyone in our path – *leave me alone, or I'll bite.*

On the third day in, I cook Limpy some whole wheat pasta and chop up a Granny Smith apple. These are treats my brother used to give him several times a week, and though I have little energy to feed myself, I feel the strong urge to coax this bird in. I distract him with a peanut on the opposite end of the cage, open the door, and put a small mound of pasta and apple chunks on top of his bird food. I step back. "Wanna treat, Dimpers?" I ask.

I sit on the couch and watch him pull one brown noodle at time. He stands over the bowl on one foot, while the other foot grabs a long strand of pasta. He nibbles and pieces fall in the cracks of his wire cage. He finishes one strand and grabs for another. The noodle hangs momentarily like a worm from his mouth while he adjusts his stance. I leave the room with some comfort knowing he is now eating.

Within a few days Limpy starts to talk. His voice sounds comfortingly like my brother's, but he is also quickly picking up the unique voices of our house. He calls me mom in Trea's voice. He answers every ringing phone with Jessica's hello.

The bird is becoming a part of our family, and it doesn't take long to realize he will be staying. Every night I turn off the overhead in the living room saying, "Good night, Dimpers."

"Good night, Dimpers," he now whispers back, mimicking my voice — not my brother's — as I head down the hall to my bedroom.

Matt playing the guitar his
dad gave him

Tami & her dad in
Charleston, 2002

Steve and his guitar
at the beach

Godiva Girl

The house feels as cold as it did a few days ago when we picked up the bird. Matt and Tami wanted to come back over before heading to Charleston the next morning, so here the three of us are.

As soon as we walk in the door, we separate. Each of us goes toward the place in the house that seems to be calling to us. Tami moves toward the dining room where Steve has a collection of photos on a trifold screen. Matt goes to the front bedroom he and Tami shared when they came up to visit their dad. I feel like a stranger, as if I'm roaming around someone's house without permission. I move through the dining room and the hall to Steve's bedroom.

I sit on the edge of Steve's unmade bed, watching down the hall as Tami moves into the bedroom with her brother. The house is small and almost a hundred years old, so from the bed I have a perfect view of the kids. They travel around the room collecting things they want. I watch as a small mound grows near their door in the hallway. Their hearts are empty and they are trying to fill them with pieces of their dad.

Matt is almost fourteen. He is so much his father's son — quiet and sensitive, balanced with a subtle sense of humor. He and his dad would walk through department stores and hockey-check one another into racks of clothes. They'd watch silly movies and rewind when there was one particular line that struck them as funny. That line was replayed even in their everyday exchanges, just a shared moment of silliness that no one else would get.

I grab Steve's pillow and bury my face in it, breathing in his last night's sleep in this place. Sobs are silent and pressed hard against the feathery pillow. I think maybe I'll never wash these sheets. Matt walks toward me, and I straighten myself up.

"What will happen with everything else?"

"Well, your dad would want you two to have whatever you want, so maybe in a few months Doug and I can rent a truck and bring the things you want down to Charleston. We'll need to talk to your mom about where you can store furniture, but I'm sure your dad would love it if you furnished your first place with this stuff."

"I want the leather couch," Tami says walking in on us.

"That's fine, Tam. I'm sure that will be fine. For now why don't you guys just focus on taking a few things with you."

She'll miss the visits here with her dad. Tami had grown to enjoy the hiking, the camping, the canoeing. She had learned, right alongside Jess, that one *could* survive without a hair straightener for a night by a winter campfire in the mountains. Bits of her dad — leather sofa, pictures, clothing, whatnots — are all that she'll take home.

Tami walks over to the antique dresser and opens the top drawer. I hate that she is doing that. No one should touch his things. They are his. There should be no discussion of who gets what. One after the other she opens the drawers while I sit on the bed, part of me hoping they'll save a little piece of him for me. She tosses T-shirt after T-shirt onto the foot of the bed.

"This was one of his favorite shirts," she says and throws it on the bed while Matt sits on the end of the weight bench.

"Do you think I can have the weight bench? I mean, if Mom says it's okay." His teenage voice cracks slightly. He looks like a brown version of his dad. His mom is from Guam, and from her, Matt got beautiful dark hair and skin. His eyes are his dad's — soft and thoughtful. There's something about the way he carries himself that will no doubt be a constant reminder of the man we lost.

"You can have anything you want, Matty. I promise, I'll hold on to everything." But part of me wants to keep every last thing for myself. Maybe I don't count because

I'm just the sister.

"Here, Therese." Tami tosses a T-shirt toward me. "Oh, this was definitely one of his favorites. He wore it all the time."

"Thanks, Tam." I hold the T-shirt up in front of me. *Save the Rainforest* it says, and it has a picture of random jungle animals circling the words. "He did wear this a lot. Are you sure you don't want it? Matt, how about you?" I'm praying he'll say I can keep it. He does, and I'm grateful.

Matt gets up and comes to sit by me, while Tami moves to the closet. Her long brown hair is pulled into a tight ponytail that swishes back and forth when she walks. She is beautiful and exotic just like her mom.

With Steve's pillow still pushed down in my lap, Matt and I sit side by side on the bed watching Tami. I grab a wooden box from the nightstand and open it. "Look at this," I say and pull a signed guitar pick from the miscellaneous items hiding in the box.

Matt takes it from my hand and tries to read the signature. "Who is it?"

"Edwin McCain," I say and lean further into Matt.

"Man, Dad loved Edwin McCain. How'd he get the pick?"

"This past summer we saw Edwin play at Visulite. You know, the theater right around the corner." I point toward the back of the house and spin back around. "After the show, your dad, Doug, and I waited to see if Edwin might come out to sign autographs, and when the place was nearly empty, he did. You know, your dad and I had seen him before at the Peace Center in Greenville a few years back. That was a much bigger show though, so not really an opportunity for autographs. Anyway, Edwin came out, took a few pictures with starstruck older women, and then talked to us." Matt and I are both looking at the pick as if it is telling us the story.

"We told him how much we enjoyed the show. Your dad told him he had just learned one of his songs on guitar. Just a really nice guy. So, we talked for a few minutes, and I asked for an autograph. I felt a little like a stalker, but what the hell, right?" A slow smile forms on Matt's face. "I handed him a matchbook, and he said *hold on*. He fished in his pocket. *Only one*, he said as he pulled this pick out. I thought your dad would fall over. The look on his face. So, Edwin signs the pick and hands it to me. Your dad looked at me like I'd just stolen his candy."

"Very cool," Tami interjects from the closet.

"I mean, funny isn't it? Your dad's the big fan. He's the one who plays guitar, not me. So I thank Edwin, and the three of us walk away. The second we were out of earshot your dad leans in and whispers, *you're definitely giving me that pick*. On the walk home I danced around in front of him dangling the pick. *Maybe I'll play guitar*, I said as we headed down the sidewalk. Of course, by the time we were home, I gave him the pick." I look at Matt. The hours his dad spent at Matt's guitar lessons. The parental nudges for practice. The two of them playing a John Cougar song together last summer. "You play guitar; he'd want you to have it. Please don't lose it, Matt," I say and wrap his hand firmly around the pick.

"I won't," he says and stands to stuff it in his jeans

pocket. "Wonder what's under the bed." He stoops down and flips the brown comforter up over the side.

"Don't know." I meet him on the floor.

Matt pulls a roll of red wrapping paper and two un-wrapped white boxes from under the bed. "What's this?" He sets the boxes on the bed.

Tami finds her way over from the pile of clothes and shoes she's now created on the floor outside the closet. The three of us surround the boxes on the bed. We look at each other, then at the boxes. "For Shana? Should we open them?" Tami asks.

Steve died two days before Valentine's, and he and Shana were supposed to go out for dinner, some Italian restaurant she loved.

"Let's open them," I say and wonder if that's the right thing.

Tami slides her finger under the tape holding down the lid of the larger of the two boxes. She pulls the white tissue paper back to reveal a soft floral peasant shirt. "Dad bought this for Shana at a shop by The Battery when he came down to Charleston a few weeks ago." Tami folds the paper back over and puts the box to the side. She opens the other box, and as soon as the white lid lifts I see a smaller brown box.

I pick up the box and hold it, rubbing my fingers across the embossed font — *Godiva Chocolatier*.

Last Valentine's Day Steve was interested in a girl who worked at a neighborhood restaurant he frequented. The girl, Kris, had jerked him around a bit. One minute she wanted to go out with him, and the next she was too busy. One minute she was sick of guys who treated her like shit, the next she was dating guys who treated her like shit. "You're too good for her," I said.

He called me. "I'm going to get her some Godiva chocolates for Valentine's. You know, take them to her at work."

"You're crazy," I said carrying the phone to my mail-box. "You don't give just *any* girl Godiva chocolates. Not all women are Godiva worthy. Kris is more of a Whitman Sampler kind of girl."

"Really? Are you sure?" he asked.

"Trust me. I'm sure," I said and that was that. Kris got the sampler, and Steve moved on within a few weeks.

When Steve started seeing Shana a few months ago, I was thrilled. He had known her from a distance and through friends for almost two years. She was a local singer and songwriter who had been voted "Best Female Voice" by *Creative Loafing*. Because of past unhealthy relationships with men, Shana was incredibly slow to move their relationship to the next level. Steve would call me after one of their dates and go through a play by play of *he said, she saids* to get a big sister's perspective on whether Shana was really interested in him. There was a refreshing innocence to their time together — late night talks, guitar strumming.

Steve's death really rocked Shana's world. "I wasn't confident enough to really give myself to him. I would have, you know?" she said the day of his funeral. At the service, she'd sung one of Steve's favorite songs, *Forever*.

"He knew," I said and brushed the heavy blond

ringlets off her shoulders as we stood on my parents' front porch.

Now I'm holding her truth — *you are worth it* — in a red-bowed Godiva box.

"Godiva girl," I say out loud, still holding the box.

Tami looks at me like I have lost my mind. "You okay?"

"Fine. I'm fine." I grab the red tube of wrapping paper from the floor. "I'm just going to wrap these for Shana."

Dealing With It

Steve & Dad on a hunting trip, 1986

Steve & Mom, 1970

Playing Monopoly,
December 1977

Inmate

He sits across the courtroom, his back to me, bouncing that orange-jumpsuited leg nervously. My brother used to do that. The shackles shake and clink like keys every time his leg moves. INMATE is written in big bold black letters across his back. A purple shadow circles his left eye, and I think maybe this is something he's earned in a jail cell. Dirty blond spikes of hair surround his angular face. He looks like one of those police sketches released on the evening news, and I can't stop glaring at him.

My stomach hurts. I haven't eaten for two days, as if fasting will make this crazy ride stop. I imagine myself jumping the bar in a fit of rage and pounding the killer's unaffected face until he is unrecognizable. Then I contemplate the consequences, which is more than he'd done a few weeks ago when he put a gun to Steve's chest and pulled the trigger. I glance around the room trying to spot his family but have no idea who I'm looking for. No one seems too concerned with him, or for that matter, anything in the courtroom.

I fix my eyes back on him. At twenty-two, he looks like a little boy sitting between the two attorneys in dark suits. I wonder what his childhood was like, and if in his wildest dreams he ever imagined himself killing another human being.

My parents came down last night and now they sit beside me arguing over whether or not they should have left the dog in the hotel room alone. "Richard," my mom whispers through gritted teeth, "you need to call the hotel because if we're not back in time they may send someone to clean the room."

Thank God I opted to drive down this morning.

"I'm sure the dog will be fine," I interject across my dad.

"People have been known to steal dogs before, Therese."

"Mother, I really don't think anyone is staking out your hotel room to steal Miss Kitty. Isn't being here to address the judge more important than that damn dog?" I hate my tone as soon as the words leave my mouth, but patience, at this point, I save like a gift for special occasions and noisy kids.

My mom sits back, and I think she is done, but she leans across my dad again. "Are you heading straight back or do you want to get some lunch?"

"I think I'll head straight back," I say. "I have a lot to do this afternoon."

"State verses Karl Staton," the young woman announces.

The prosecutor stands and motions toward us. "The victim's family is present, Your Honor. If it pleases the court, the parents and older sister would like to make a brief statement."

Joe couldn't do it, he'd said. After years inside the system, he just couldn't bring himself to sit in a courtroom.

"Well, I think that would be perfectly accept-able." The judge nods like a sympathetic grandfather. "I appreciate your being here today and am sorry for your loss. Please approach the bench."

The three of us stand and walk beyond the bar and the well-dressed important people scattered across the front of the room. Tonya, the victim advocate, has coached us on addressing the judge, so we have some idea of the protocol. Brief, she said. Be brief.

"Your Honor," I start, "I am the older sister of the victim. I cannot work, sleep, or eat since my brother's murder. I would ask that you at least give me the peace of knowing Karl Staton will remain behind bars until his trial. Thank you, Your Honor."

Then my mother speaks, and my father, but their words are muffled because I have a clear view of Karl to my right. Like a scolded child, he sits, chin down, staring at his lap.

And as abruptly as it began, it ends. "Karl Staton your bond is set at..." The judge speaks and his voice carries on, but all I hear is *twenty-five-thousand dollars*. The three of us turn and walk toward Tonya, who is holding the bar's gate open. We file out of the courtroom, and the people sitting in neat rows watch us. The deputy opens the door, and we step out, and I realize this is one piece of this new reality I can mark off my "to do" list.

The prosecutor and one of the detectives from the case walk out behind us. "Can I talk to you a minute?" I ask as soon as the door closes behind them. The prosecutor nods and the detective opens the door to a small conference room in the foyer right outside of the courtroom.

"I'll be right out. Give me a minute," I tell my parents and I step in.

The door barely closes behind Detective Bailey. "I want to see his statement. The killer's statement," I say, rounding the little table and taking a seat.

Bailey leans tall and black against the white wall. He could pass for a model or a primetime-TV-show cop. His confidence borders on arrogance, a trait I've always despised but in this instance find rather comforting. Without a word, he stoops over to grab the old briefcase that leans, like him, against the wall.

Ms. Townsend, the prosecutor, sits down beside me and glances toward the detective. "Hang on. I have it right here." She is young and sports a preppy brunette bob, a navy suit, and sensible shoes. She flips nervously through the black binder that holds the remnants of my brother's existence.

"You would have dated him," I say, trying to convince her he is worth fighting for. She stops, holding one of the pages up and turns toward me.

A knock on the door startles us out of the moment. Townsend drops the page open and pushes her chair back to go to the door. Bailey holds out a hand to stop her. "I got it," he says and hurries around the table to catch the interruption.

The binder lies beside me — a morbid invitation — and I glance down to see the autopsy photos spread over two pages. And before anyone notices, my eyes are drawn to the vision of his body. His naked body lies blue-grey on that silver platter table. He looks like the CPR dummy in Mr. Steen's sixth-grade health class. The one that the students would take turns blowing air into, our mouths touching the cold lips over and over until we got our A. Only, unlike that dummy, he has a small dark hole in the center of his chest.

I want to cover my little brother, to save his already lost dignity, to warm a body long cold. My mind slips into childhood, and I imagine us both in footed pajamas crawling around a shag carpet during Saturday morning cartoons. I want to bicker, and jump ramps with our bikes, and step on bees in a front yard full of clover, and go on imaginary trips together in my grandfather's Pontiac, where I always hogged the driver's seat.

I release Steve to the prosecutor's hand and look at the detective. "I want directions. Tell me how to get to the club," I say as if I'm the one heading up this investigation. "I can read the statement later."

"Are you sure you want to do that?" His voice sounds like a caring older brother. "That may not be such a good idea."

"I'm sure."

"I'll drive you," he says. "It's not a good idea for you to go there alone."

Ms. Townsend watches us like a movie she wants no part in.

I push back from the table. "Let's go then."

"If you have any questions," the prosecutor says, "call me anytime. We don't want you to feel like because you're two hours away, we are not working on this." She hands me her card, and the three of us file out of the room.

In the hall, my parents stand with their backs toward us, staring into a black-and-white photo that hangs in a series on the tidy courthouse walls. I wonder where their minds are. In the past few weeks it seems they have aged rapidly.

If parents have favorites, then Steve was my mother's. I mean from the time he was little. He was the easiest kid if nothing else. Never a problem at school. Never a problem at home. Easy.

When Steve was a teenager, he got into the martial arts thing. He met a guy at the gym who taught, and before long he and several of his buddies had an all-out dojo every Sunday afternoon in the room right above our dining room. My mom would be cooking Sunday's pasta and setting the table under the stomps and kicks and punches that swayed the dining room chandelier. Dad wasn't crazy about all the ruckus, but he tolerated it. My mom embraced it. "Leave them alone, Richard," she'd say and then she'd feed whoever stayed after.

Dad will turn seventy this year. He has far outlived

his youngest son. I know how much he misses Steve. Not because he talks about it but because they were friends. When Steve was in junior and senior high, he and my dad spent hours in the woods together hunting.

My dad would take a big group of guys camping or hunting even though he was neither a camper nor a hunter in traditional terms. Unless drinking coffee and eating cold pizza sprinkled with garlic while sitting right under my brother's tree stand was to be considered real hunting. Steve would spend hours preparing for the hunt — dousing himself with deer urine, washing his clothes in baking soda to make sure he had no human scent. And then undoubtedly my dad, between naps, would spot the biggest buck in the woods.

They had been friends.

I stand behind my parents, praying they won't want to tag along.

Tonya, the victim advocate, walks around the corner and answers my prayer. "I'd like to talk to you for a minute," she says, stopping nearest my mother.

I only met her briefly before entering the courtroom, but it is my understanding that it is her job to be nice to my family. Mother already had her cornered this morning.

"Sure," my mom says, "did I tell you the joke about the blonde and the rowboat?"

This is my mother. In the days of crowds swarming our house after Steve's death, my mother sat at the dining room table entertaining. Telling joke after joke, laughing, smoking, eating. I know she'd rather melt down, but I'm not sure she can. Maybe it's fear. Maybe it's inability. Maybe it's unwillingness. All I know is that it is my mother.

"Nope, I don't think you've shared that one, Betty."

"Well, I'm going to head out," I say and try to pull away from my parents, knowing today Tonya is earning her money.

My mom grabs my arm. "Wait, you haven't heard this one."

"I think I have. Besides, I'm going by the police station for a minute to talk to Detective Bailey. I'll talk to you this afternoon." I pull away, and my mom grabs

Tonya's arm.

"I don't think she's heard it, but I'll tell her later," she whispers, leaning in toward Tonya.

"You guys be safe, and don't forget the dog."

Dad smiles. "We won't," he says as I walk away.

When we pull up to the club, Detective Bailey tells me step by step exactly what happened, and where, in the parking lot. I scan the lot, and feel for my brother's presence but know this is hardly the place he'd be hanging around now.

A construction crew works on the roof right above the front door. Only a few cars in the lot and I can't help but think about the men who sit just inside the building. I imagine leather chairs, and the smell of alcohol. Sticky poles, and stickier women twirling from them. I hate that this is where my little brother met God, but it is.

"I'm ready. I still want to see the statement."

"Let's go back to the station. You can read the statement, and then I'll take you back to get your car over at the courthouse. Good?"

"Yep."

We pull away, and somehow I feel like I'll come back here later. Not because my brother is here because he isn't, but because I want to go inside. I want to be in the place where he was in those last moments of his life. The fact that it's a strip club doesn't change this desire.

The station is loud and desks seemed to be piled one on the other. We walk through detectives on phones, gathered two and three around, drinking coffee from thick mugs. "Let's go in my office, and I'll set you up with the whole file."

I sit at a battered old desk while Bailey goes to get the file.

He returns with a binder much like the prosecutor's. He flips it open. "Table of contents here. You can see the statements are all in order — Karl's, witnesses'. Want some coffee or something?"

"Nope. I'm good."

"Take your time."

Bailey walks out and leaves me with the binder. I

know the pictures are here, so I cautiously turn through the first few pages to get to Karl's statement. It's confusing, and I'm not sure if that's because of Karl or because of all the spelling and grammatical errors. I'm assuming this is the norm. I can't imagine a bunch of cops sitting around with red pens and dictionaries after they've completed interviews with killers and drug dealers and victims of crime.

Foster care until he was almost five. Abuse. Hospitalization. Graduated from high school in the same county I teach in. A younger sister. She's a stripper. He's been a stripper. Girlfriend also a stripper. He was there watching her strip. Dated about three weeks. She wouldn't let him leave after he shot Steve.

I close the binder. I'm exhausted. It's been a few weeks now since this kid killed my brother and landed in a jail in Greenville. I wonder what happened to the girlfriend, to the sister.

I walk out of the office and spot Bailey talking to a uniformed cop. As soon as he sees me, he cuts his conversation and walks over.

"You okay?"

"Yep. His life." I feel a conflict growing in me.

"Pretty crazy, huh? There's more." Bailey walks past me and grabs the binder. "Still a punk. You ready to get out of here?"

"Yes."

I head straight for the interstate. Driving, I fumble through my purse for a pen and my pad. Thoughts race circles. I find the pad and hold it on the steering wheel long enough to write a few lines. My body starts shaking and the image of my brother on the silver table surfaces. I pull off the road to call Doug.

He answers, "You okay?"

"Maybe I'm not supposed to hate him. I don't want to hate him. Does that make me a bad sister? Does that mean I didn't truly love my brother? I didn't love him enough?"

"Hate who? What are you talking about?"

"The guy. The guy who killed Steve," I respond through tears.

"No, Therese. I think that means you loved your brother *more* than you thought you did."

I hang up and sit staring out the windshield. Traffic whizzes by, and I sit, hands on the steering wheel, tears dropping into my lap on the shoulder of I-85.

Steve backpacking
in the late 1990's

Steve & Therese
Beach trip, 1999

Matt & his dad on the
Appalachian Trail

It Sucks

Blue ball cap pulled down over my eyes and pajamas still on, I push a cart aimlessly down the aisles of the Winn Dixie near our house. I haven't bathed since the bond hearing two days ago, and frankly, I don't give a shit how I look.

Steve worked in the dairy department of Harris Teeter when he was in high school. I'd take Jessica in to shop when I knew Steve was working. *Chick magnet*, he used to say about her. Girls love babies. This did seem to be true until Steve decided to ask out a cashier who thought I was his wife and Jess was his baby. That all worked out when I marched up there to explain my little brother wasn't cheating on me — the little wife at home with a toddler. He dated the girl, Rebecca, for a little over a year.

"Mrs. B?" I hear from behind me. "Mrs. B, is that you?"

I turn, recognizing the voice as Michael, one of my favorite students.

He walks over, Winn Dixie's blue apron over his school clothes. "When are you coming back to school? Our sub sucks. You wouldn't believe the freak'n Gatsby project she has us working on."

I don't have the nerve to tell him I'll likely never come back. A few people have said *gotta get back in there, back in life, back in a routine, back to normal.* But I don't have a clue what normal means. I can't fathom it — routine, jumping back in there. I feel like maybe my insides are raw and exposed to the world, and the truth is, I don't trust this world.

I feign interest with a nod, but he sees through me and something shifts.

"I'm gonna help you shop," he says and puts his

heavy arm around me. At six-foot-three, he looks down on me, seeing me more like a little sister than his high school English teacher. Michael, at seventeen, gets grief. His mother died of cancer only a few months back, and not quite a year ago, his older brother was killed in a car accident the day after graduation. Now all that is left of his brother is a white wooden cross in the median of Highway 74.

Michael holds on to my cart the way my kids used to when they were little, and we circle the aisles together. When I stop to grab something he waits patiently behind me. "Which one?" he says when I stand in front of a shelf of dog food. I point, and he heaves the big bag to the bottom of my cart. We walk on together.

"It sucks doesn't it?" he says, watching me stare into the cellophane window on a pasta box as if an answer would be there. "It just sucks," he repeats.

I look up. Dark brown bangs sweep to one side of a face that will someday belong to a handsome man. We smile at each other in silence on aisle four.

"All baggers to the front, please. All baggers to the front."

"I better get back up front," he says.

"How are you so happy, Michael? You're always smiling. I don't get it. Are you really happy?"

He pulls me close under one arm. "You'll be okay," he says and looks down at me still holding the pasta. He grabs the box from my hand and tosses it into the cart. "I promise. You'll be okay," he says, squeezes me, and walks away.

Uncle Steve took Jessica fishing

Jess & her uncle
on the beach

Steve holding Jess & Trea
1989

Kicking the Habit

At a little after midnight Doug kicks me out of bed. He says he can't take the squirming anymore. Since I was a kid, when I can't sleep I'll move my legs scissor-like across the sheets on the bottom of the bed. Tonight, I admit, all-out wiper blades are going back and forth. Back and forth.

First, I try reading a book, then I contemplate opening a bottle of wine. I flip through the gamut of cable channels, and every time the channel changes, Limpy clicks. He sounds like an old man with food stuck in his teeth. I tell him he is making me crazy, but he just says *okay* and keeps on clicking.

Ten minutes later, I stand, flannel pajama-clad

(pajamas are my favorite clothes), leaning across the cluttered counter at the Circle K a mile from our house. Tonight I have decided to start smoking — a little something to take the edge off.

It's been two weeks since I quit my job. I only made it through a week of classes. It just didn't feel right being there. The two honors classes were the real problem. Every day, those hungry ninth-grade eyes stared up at me as if I could possibly impart knowledge. I had nothing to give them. Nothing.

My students are hardly the only ones I've deserted. When the little kids come, I walk through the motions, unattached. I want to love them. I want to be the stepmom they need, but I'm numb.

Jess and Trea continue to wander through days in their own private grief. We're all careful for the most part except on nights like last night when the insides get out.

Jessica stormed up the stairs to the den. "You're not my dad," she screamed in Doug's face. And he's not, so he stood back silent while she spit the words at him.

She swung her arms wildly when he didn't react. He tried to stop her from crying and swinging by grabbing her in a hug while he peacocked his head back and sideways to avoid potential blows. I ran into the den to pull her away, but she backed up on her own. All the while whimpering, "You're not Steve. You're not my dad." Streaks of black mascara ran down her face like she was some kind of monster. She took off down the stairs and out the front door. Her Mustang sped down the driveway while Doug and I stood under the porch light.

But that was last night. Tonight, the cigarette packets are in neat colorful rows behind the clerk.

"What can I get you, little lady?" His gray hair is parted to one side and slicked down with some kind of shiny something.

"Not sure."

He doesn't know it's my first time.

In junior high school I tried smoking a few times, but it never seemed to work out right. To me there was nothing cool about hovering over a toilet in a stall, coughing with two or three girls in Catholic school uniforms. Nothing cool.

"Let me know." He half sits on the wooden stool in front of the register and crosses his arms over the dark blue smock — the name *Larry* written on a cockeyed nametag right above the red embroidered Circle K.

The doors slide open and ding as an older black man walks in and heads straight to the magazine rack against the wall.

"Capri. I'll take the Capris." Slim, ladylike box. Perfect. "Oh, let me grab a Coke." I know I'll need a chaser. I walk over to the cooler and grab a can.

Cockeyed-nametag Larry slides the cigarettes toward me, and I feel a twinge of guilt as if maybe I'm still wearing that Catholic school uniform. But I pay and the doors slide and ding as I leave.

Sitting in the Expedition right in front of the store, I hold the cigarettes between me and the steering wheel, pulling on the skinny pink strand that circles the flowered box. The cellophane wrap gets tossed on the seat beside me. I smack the box hard against the palm of one hand because I understand that's what you're supposed to do. Four or five hard smacks and I'm ready. I push the dashboard lighter in and pop my Coke open to wait.

The lighter pops out and I pull a cigarette toward my mouth. I puff hard on the cigarette and watch the red rings of flame until I'm lit. I gag on the first drag, but the Coke soothes my throat, and I balance the cigarette out a sliver of open window. I pull down the visor mirror to see myself full on. I take another tiny puff, exhale out the cracked window, tiny puff, exhale, tiny puff, exhale. The cigarette doesn't seem to get any smaller, and I'm not feeling great.

Cigarette poised between my index and middle finger, I crank the car and back out. I drive toward the house in this awkward puff-exhale-drink, puff-exhale-drink rhythm of my new habit. The cigarette burns low only a few blocks from the house. I haven't thought this through, and it's getting pretty close to the filter. The ashtray is filled with spare change, and I'm about to get burned, so I try to shove the cigarette out the crack. It gets caught, so I roll down the window, but my Capri lands in my lap. I slam on the brakes and wiggle under the burn until I'm able to catch it and toss it wholly out the window.

I pull down the driveway right in front of the trash can, gather my purse, cigarettes, and Coke. When I get out, the cold air makes me feel a little nauseated. I take a sip of Coke, toss the can in the red recycling bin and the Capris into the trash.

When I get in bed, Doug rolls instinctively toward me. An arm and a leg flop over me. "You okay?" he asks, and his face is nuzzled into my cheek.

"Yep. Fine."

He breathes me in. "You smell like smoke."

"That's weird." I turn my back toward him. "I quit smoking tonight." I murmur.

He wraps tight around me, a sigh of sleepy warm breath in my hair.

Matt & Trea on a back-
packing trip with Steve

Joe, Therese, Mom & Dad

Matt, Tami, Jess & Trea
2001

Coffee Shop God

Two months after the funeral, our lives have slipped uneasily into a new normal. My niece and nephew have gone back to Charleston with the knowledge that they will now live their lives without their father. From my bedroom, I can still hear my two teenagers busying themselves downstairs. My four stepchildren sleep without real understanding of the grief that cloaks our house.

Steve and I spent hours splashing through mud puddles with our mouths open. Raindrops pricking our tongues like a giant sprinkler. He was only three weeks old when my mom found my toddler body wrapped around his in a tiny bassinet. We slept in the same bed until I was nearly thirteen. Not because we didn't both have our own beds, but because that was where we felt at home. He never seemed to mind that most nights I'd wet us both and we'd have to relocate.

With one phone call, my little brother became a permanent *was* in my life, and tonight I just can't face it. I can't grasp the concept of him as past tense — a phase like bangs or an ex-boyfriend.

So, here I lie with my new husband. I resent him for being alive. I resent God's wicked timing, giving me one man only months before taking the other.

"Where is he?" I ask.

"In heaven," he responds half asleep. "He's in heaven."

I sit up. "What does that mean? I don't think you're understanding me. *Where is my brother right now*? I mean, what is he doing — eating, hiking, sitting by a stream?"

"I don't know." He sighs heavily. It is obvious he is beginning to understand the line I have drawn somewhere down the middle of the bed. He knows better than to give me some canned biblical response about golden streets and flowing rivers. So he sits up beside me in the dark until I give up and fall back into the sheets.

I lie in self-inflicted isolation pondering the after-life. The whole *better place with God* concept has lost all conceivable merit. I just want my brother back. I want the gunshot to miss his heart. I want to take back the night of the phone call, the panic, and the shocking news that traveled across states waking the people who loved him. But it isn't like when we were kids; there are no take backs. It is done. He is done.

I wake with the same heaviness. No revelations in my sleep, no comforting dreams, just grief's weight gluing me to the bed. A feeling that sucks the air out of the room. I close my eyes and pray my life has been a dream until now.

With the sheet over my head like a little girl, I look down toward my body and the T-shirt I got from Steve's things a few weeks back. The same T-shirt I've been wearing for two days. *Rainforest* spelled out in big letters across my chest, almost fluorescent under the white sheet. *Fuck the rainforest – save me.*

I throw back the sheet and sit up. I know if I don't get out of bed, depression, like a lover, will convince me to stay.

I hear the kids and the cartoons and all the usual sounds of chaos that fill our Sunday morning house. So, I dress quickly, kiss Doug goodbye, and head for the coffee shop.

The ten-minute drive gives me time to bargain with God. *I need a sign*, I plead. *God, let me make this infinitely clear. I don't want some little subtle heavenly maybe. I want flashing neon and audible voices. I need something big, something that will give me a sense of hope. A reason to stay alive.*

I miss the usual Sunday morning pre-church coffee crowd. A table against the wall is free, so armed with my journal and the Bible I was given a couple of months before Steve's death, I head over and set my stuff down. I grab a coffee and settle in. I begin writing but am interrupted by a man's voice coming from behind me.

"Mr. Reynolds, I really need you to call me. It's important. I'm trying to plan my son's funeral, and I need..." His voice drifts off.

Funeral. His son.

My heart and my pencil drop. I have the overwhelming desire to spin around and console this stranger. I need to help him, or commiserate, or wallow in his sorrow. What can I possibly say to him? I can choose from one of the many inappropriate, insufficient responses: *All things happen for good. God only gives us what we can handle. What doesn't kill us makes us stronger.* These are lines of the unaffected, and we're not part of that group.

I pick up my pencil but can't write. I have to think of something, some way to comfort this father. I flip open my Bible hoping to find the perfect passage, but all I keep thinking is, what if I say the wrong thing? What if what I say hurts him more than saying nothing?

Am I missing it – God's green light, flashing obnoxious neon colors like Vegas at night?

I have to see him. At least be able to give grief in the coffee shop a face. I stand and grab my cup for a refill. When I turn toward the counter and him, I'm surprised by how young he is. Early thirties. Maybe. Slim and earthy like my brother. His son must have been young. He sits alone staring into a cup of coffee as if it holds the answers. He clasps his cell phone tightly in one hand as if to hold on to what is left of life.

As I walk past him, guts spinning, I have the urge to hug him.

Instead I clear my throat in an attempt to get his attention. He doesn't look up. I refill my coffee and return to my seat.

I try to let it go, let him go. Try to refocus on my journal, but I'm obsessed with this man and what we share.

I convince myself I'll wait for that perfect moment to address him.

His chair moves against the wood floor. My stomach knots. He walks past me, and I want to grab him, but I lose my courage. A flush of shame covers me, as if I've somehow let down this stranger.

But he hesitates, stops, and sits down at the table directly in front of me. My mind races with excitement and awe that this is God's neon sign.

"Sir." I clear my throat, and speak up, "I'm sorry."

He turns toward me, and I rush to fill any chance of an awkward silence between us. "I'm sorry about your son. I couldn't help but overhear you. I just lost my brother."

That last part is the key. *I lost my brother.* I get it.

The man's eyes soften.

"Can I do anything for you?" I need to ask even though I know nothing I can ever do will relieve his agony. "How old was he?"

"He died on Thursday in delivery. My first child." He whispers, staring into the wooden table. "The umbilical cord strangled him."

"And your wife. How is she?"

"She's still in the hospital. I had to get out of there to do some planning. She doesn't seem to want me around anyway. Her sister is with her. I have to go to the funeral home tonight. I just want to go sit with him."

His eyes swell with tears. He is broken, and I want to help fix him.

I move to the chair beside him. We lean toward each other as if we have a secret.

"My brother Steve died almost three weeks ago."

"What happened?"

"He was shot. Wrong place, wrong time. And now I'm not sure who to be." I almost break down. "Or for that matter, how to be." I breathe in heavy and maintain composure.

He stares into me, and I realize he's probably found some comfort in just knowing someone else's world has just been shattered. I'm okay with this.

"God, I'm sorry," he says. "I know what you mean. I already had plans for him. He would have played sports — probably baseball. We'd go camping and fishing. You know, all that guy stuff. Aaron. His name was Aaron."

His face lowers as if he's suddenly realized his son and all that he'd hoped for him has passed. "Now, I don't know. He wasn't baptized. Do you think he's in heaven? Do you think your brother is in heaven? Do you believe there is a heaven?"

I hear myself in his voice: unsure, wanting — no needing — answers.

"Yes, he's in heaven." I smile and continue, *"They're* in heaven. My brother loves kids. I'll bet they're hiking a beautiful mountain. I'll bet Steve is teaching him to fish the way you would have. They see us, but don't miss us." Words fly confidently from my mouth. No time to question, or believe. "Not because they've forgotten us or don't love us, but because this life is only a blink. They don't have time to miss us."

"Can I pray with you?" I say, completely uncharacteristic of the woman I am or the woman I was or the woman I thought I was. I've never prayed in public.

"Yes." He leans closer to me, and the world drops away when I clasp this father's hands in mine and pray with him, knee to knee in the coffee shop ten minutes from my house.

When I release him, we stand, and I picture him sitting alone in front of a tiny casket. Part of me knows that someday he will have another child, but never a replacement. I collect my things, and we walk outside together.

"It sucks," I say, and grab his hand one last time. A slow smile forms on his broken face, and I hug him.

"But we'll be okay," I whisper and let him go.

MOVING ON

Steve & Therese on her
wedding day, November
2002

Tami & Matt on a
camping trip with their dad

Jessica & Uncle Steve
1988

Sisters

The benches, like Sunday's pews, creak and settle as we file into our seats in the packed courtroom. Karl pled to voluntary manslaughter with a twenty-year maximum.

The Greenville solicitor told us a few months back this was the way to go. "We can't chance what a jury would do with this case," she said. Strip club and the Bible Belt — not a good mix. Jurors might well see this as a shouldn't-have-been-in-a-place-like-that kind of thing. As if none of them had ever gone home with a pocket full of two-dollar bills and some stripper's breath on their necks. This Bible-induced hypocrisy strikes me hard. But it is what it is, so we're here for the sentencing, and for the opportunity to address the judge.

My stomach rumbles loud enough to hear over the chatter of onlookers and criminals and attorneys and bailiffs. I haven't eaten since breakfast yesterday, and I feel like I might throw up. Doug squeezes my leg, and I keep his hand there as if that may stop the churning.

"You okay?" he asks.

He looks good in the same black suit he wore to Steve's funeral a year ago.

"Yep," I say, but I am sure he knows better.

I'm pretty sure he got more than he bargained for. "For better or worse," he keeps saying even though the worse doesn't seem to be getting better. I've tried on various new me's since Steve's death, and Doug has to be wondering which one will finally stick.

Tonya, the victim advocate, leans across Doug so I can hear her. "He'll come out over there, but not until they call the case." She points discreetly to the door on our left.

"Is his family here?" I ask and feel my mother and father lean in to eavesdrop.

"I haven't seen them yet." She hands me a small

wad of tissue and sits back, brushing against Doug.

"What did she say?" my mother asks leaning across Dad.

"Karl will come out over there." I eye the door. "His family is not here yet." I sit back straight against the hard wood and pray I can make it through this without being sick.

I survey the family. Steve's ex-wife, his daughter, and his girlfriend, Shana, are shoulder to shoulder in the row right behind us. At the last minute, Jessica decided not to come. "I can't handle it, Mom," she said yesterday, rubbing her hand up and down the cat's back. "I'm afraid I'll do something to him. Afraid I'll lose it." And I get this. My son and Steve's are sitting at the far end of the bench closest to the door where Karl will come out, and I think maybe that wasn't a good idea. They're unforgiving teenag- ers, and the truth is they'd like to kill the man who de- stroyed our lives. I can't blame them for that.

"Tonya, do I have time to go to the bathroom?"

"We have a few minutes. They'll probably call your

case first, so hurry back."

The bathroom is empty. I shut myself in the first stall. I stand, sucking in the air of the courthouse bathroom. I'm not sure if I'll be sick, so I wait it out a few minutes. The door opens and someone moves into the stall next to mine. I flush instinctively even though I've only been taking up this space.

When I turn on the water at the sink, I remember how in elementary school sometimes I'd go to the bathroom just to use up five minutes of a boring day. I'd busy myself though — a pull on the toilet paper, an unnecessary flush, a reflective moment at the sink — and then back to class.

The water runs down over my hands, and in the mirror I can see the picture of Steve pinned to my black lapel. I made these pins yesterday. A mark of remembrance or solidarity or both. The picture was taken at my house at Christmas. Steve came over pretty early that morning for breakfast. He sat in the living room playing guitar while

Doug sang along.

A toilet flushes and takes my moment with it. The woman comes out and joins me at the next sink. I look over toward her in that awkward bathroom moment with a stranger. The slim blurry blackness of her pantsuit is all I see.

"Who's in the picture?" Her voice is hesitant over the running water.

Tiny blue cursive letters circle the white frame of my brother's picture: *Never forgotten, my brother and my friend.*

"My brother," I say and step away from the sink for a paper towel. "He was killed last year."

"Here in Greenville?" she inquires and turns off the water.

"Yes."

She studies me for a moment before meeting me over the wastebasket. Blond hair touches her cheeks softly on both sides and accentuates the slight slant of her blue eyes. That slant that I've tried for years to get using dark pencil around the outer edges of my eyes.

"I'm Karl Staton's sister, Rachel."

I swallow hard and hope someone will walk in and save me from this moment. But no one does, so we stand together in clumsy silence — two sisters dressed in black in the courthouse bathroom.

"I'm sorry," she says, and I believe her. She speaks as if she is afraid of me, afraid of my response. Afraid I will attack her alone in the bathroom. But part of me wants desperately to hug her, to comfort her like a big sister. Something about her looks vulnerable. Maybe it's her age (twenty-one), which I know from the case notes. Maybe it's that she looks like a little girl playing dress up in that dark suit. Without reply, I grab the door and hold it while she steps out. I wonder if she misses her brother as much as I miss mine.

She walks a few steps and turns back toward me. "I know you hate us."

Shocked, I reply, "No. I don't hate you. I don't hate your brother."

And I don't hate him. I wonder, as I have for almost

a year, if I'm betraying my brother. If maybe loving Steve must mean hating Karl. But I smile at her. Rachel looks relieved, as if she has just gone to confession — for herself, for her brother. In this moment, forgiveness feels tangible. Like something we both need.

Allied by grief, we turn the corner and walk toward the courtroom where we'll defend our brothers. Hers imprisoned. Mine dead.

Steve & Therese sleeping,
1972

Steve in 1974

Joe, Steve & Therese,
early 1970's

Me Too

We stand outside the Mexican restaurant, ready to head back to Charlotte. The general family vibe is relief, almost an excitement for this little piece of closure. Even though we aren't thrilled with voluntary manslaughter and a ten-year sentence, at least there will be no messy trial to endure and no chance Karl will walk away without punishment.

The kids all somehow look lighter. This meal has been their last in the town that took their dad and uncle from them. They can drive away and not come back.

I cannot deny the anger that gnaws at my stomach after hearing Rachel speak on behalf of her brother — *he is all she has; she has no other family.* I wanted her to shut her mouth and walk away sorry. Sorry. That's it.

Karl turned to address the family. To apologize. He did. Turned right around, shackled and cuffed, ten feet from our red faces. Ten feet from my son and Steve's. I trembled and shook and white-knuckled the bar. Doug leaned his body weight into mine, so I wouldn't fall over.

It is over.

My parents are leaving right after they go by the hotel. They forgot one of Miss Kitty's bowls and are hoping the maids haven't tossed it. Trea wants to ride home with Tami and Matt, who won't head back to Charleston until sometime tomorrow afternoon. This is fine with me because Shana and I want Doug to take us by the club on the way out of town.

"I'll call Joe when we get on the road," I say as my parents climb into the black Ford Focus Steve used to own. It's weird seeing them drive it.

"Ready?" Doug says.

"Yeah." I take a breath and let out a deep sigh. "I should go ahead and call him." I dig through my purse to find my cell phone.

Joe was about twelve when I woke to Steve's screaming, "I got him! Dad! Dad!"

Steve and I had been asleep in the top bunk. Joe in the bottom. Joe tried to sneak out the window, but Steve heard him. When I heard the screams, I sat up to find Steve's eight-year-old body half over the rail at the end of the bed, legs kicking, trying not to flip off. I grabbed his feet and held on while Steve pushed down tight on the window holding Joe's angry body half in and half out until my dad ran in.

I must have been in my late teens the first time Joe went to prison. Our family would all rotate visits. Steve and I went several times together to see him. The rules stick just like childhood memories: having your ID ready, not wearing anything provocative, not bringing anything unapproved to the prison — money, cigarettes, books, whatever.

Depending on the facility, sometimes we'd get a photo there in the visiting area.

So Joe answers and I tell him what happened. "Ten years. That's it."

"All right," he says and apologizes again for not coming.

When we pull up to the strip club, it's only two-thirty and there are already cars in the parking lot. The purple and white building welcomes us and any other passersby on I-85. The detective told me last year, "It's pretty upscale. Lots of businessmen." And since then, I've tried to right this notion of upscale. I mean, tits and ass, fluorescent liquor shots in beakers in the middle of the day, and girls with daddy issues slipping and sliding and twisting, untouchable. Upscale.

Doug parks the Expedition. Shana and I get out. "I'll wait here," he says and turns on the radio.

Shana wraps her arm around mine, and we walk

across the lot.

We stop and stand, for a moment, in the handi-
capped parking space. My brother had an argument with a
stranger, and here I am, a bright yellow wheelchair painted
beneath my feet. This is where Steve fell and took his last
breath. The police say he died instantly, but surely there
were seconds, just a few, when he realized he was dying.
Maybe he gasped one more breath, maybe he saw light,
maybe he regretted, or hoped, or prayed.

His killer tried to resuscitate him. His dirty mouth
on my brother's. Shocked enough to sit and wait for the
police to arrest him. Composed enough to go back into the
bar to wash Steve's blood from his hands.

Shana crouches with me. I touch the ground and
know this is a place I will never put a wreath or a flower.
Never.

"Ready?" I ask. She and I move slowly back to the
car.

When I open the car door, my cell phone is beeping.

"Your parents called." Doug hands me the phone. "I didn't pick up. You should probably call them back. Are you okay?"

"I'm fine. They can't be lost already." It's only been two days since I called my mother to let her know what I really thought of my childhood. I don't know why I got the sudden urge to point out her every fault and collectively both of their mistakes in parenting the three of us. I miss my brother, and I guess some days the void and the people he left me are just too much.

When I called my mother that morning, the answering machine picked up, and my rant began at the beep. They had never really known me; they should have been stricter — more "with it," more aware of reality. I topped it all off by pointing the finger at my dad, who had never once said he loved me.

Now the thought of that message being rewound over and over and the bitterness in my voice is unsettling, but I dial the phone. "Are you lost?"

My dad laughs, fumbling over the sounds of wind and traffic. "No, uh, I just wanted to tell you. Well, I just wanted to say that I love you. I mean I think you already knew, but, um, you did know, right?"

Caught off guard, I sit speechlessly smiling, and my heart breaks for a dad who didn't have the chance to tell his son he loved him.

I picture my dad and my mom driving only a few miles ahead of us on the highway with their windows rolled down. My mom leaning on one arm with smudged reading glasses on top of her head. My dad, windy-haired, with snap-on sunglasses, the dog perched on his arm, licking at the air.

"Me too," I say. "Me too."

AFTERWORD

We now live in my brother's house. We have since
fall of 2003. I often wonder when I'm walking across the
cold hardwood floors if maybe his feet walked this very
same path down the hall or across the dining room or to
feed the bird. The house is warm with his spirit — the life
he left behind. I plant flowers and rake leaves and pick up
twigs knowing these are things he did when he lived here.
Things have changed since he left — a cut-thru between the
kitchen and dining room, a new bathroom, extra bedroom.
I wanted enough change to make his house mine. And now
that is what it is — a different sameness hollowed out on
8th Street.

On this street, the tree that used to intimidate me
in the dark shadows of night out my grandmother's window
is now like an old friend watching over the yard, the house,
the people. This is the same street my little brother and
I used to walk down with pockets of change to buy candy
at the drugstore behind our grandparents' house. The

same street my mom walked down in pajamas as a teenager after sneaking out the bedroom window to meet her
best friend, Caroline. Since we've moved, I walk this street
almost every day.

Initially, this daily walk was of grave necessity —
there was no coffee in the house. But the walk became
ritual. The ritual got me out of bed when bed was my favorite spot, when I'd claim sickness to cover for my inability to
move forward. I'd throw on my clogs or flip-flops or Birks, a
long coat or sweat-suit jacket or nothing over my pajamas,
maybe a scarf or gloves or baseball cap pulled down over
my eyes. No teethbrushing, no hairbrushing — just me,
fresh from sleep walking toward that black coffee to fill the
hole left by my brother.

I'd walk toward the sweet smell of Sumatran beans
brewing just around the corner. There were days when I felt
guilty and the internal debate would ensue — go, not go, go,
not go and waste $2.06 on that cup. I decided my san-
ity was well worth the walk and the $2.06, so to this day
I walk along that sidewalk in pajamas or shorts or jeans

with a hat or umbrella, flip-flops or clogs, teeth brushed or not. This is my walk in my neighborhood and a piece of my brother walks with me whispering, *I can't believe you're still in pajamas.*

Six years later, I still have moments of all-out meltdown. I look at a picture a second too long, hear my nephew Matty's voice over the phone, see the beauty in an orange leaf in my front yard. I believe I will always have these moments, not just a reminder of my brother but a reminder of the fresh pain someone else might be feeling after losing someone close to them. I am grateful for the reminder.

These meltdowns don't last as long anymore. I will always miss Steve, and the truth is I can think of numerous things (and people) I would gladly trade to have him back. It's only over the past year that I've learned (am learning) to accept that anything can happen. Worrying about a potential loss — a child, a husband, a job — isn't going to prevent the loss. Fear is the truest opposite of faith. I *force* myself to choose faith every day.

About the time the essays stopped coming, I sat straight up in bed and informed my husband I'd be making a documentary. "Okay," he said, brushing a hand against the small of my back and falling back to sleep. So, I got out of bed and sent an e-mail to Craig, a writer friend. The biggest problem, among the many, was that I didn't have a camera. Craig did. He said, "I'm in," and along with his brother, Chris, we had an initial meeting in 2004 — only months after the sentencing hearing.

There were no storyboards; there was no real plan. We just started filming. We knew that the story was a given and that we would begin filming without thought of a steadfast plan; we agreed to let the project shape itself. Very naïve to say the least, but the truth is that it started the ball rolling. I sincerely believe if I had gotten caught up in that whole *I have no clue what I'm doing* thing, the project would have never gotten off the ground. I believe had it not been for my husband and his unwavering support and for people around me like Craig and Chris, who committed without question, the idea would have ended with me sitting straight up in bed.

But that's not what happened. In the spring of 2006, I headed to the coffee shop to meet my writers' group. I walked in to find I was one of two early comers, and the other, Tamara (also working on what we believed would someday be a film), was discussing our reservation of the meeting space with two young men. The two were in the process of storyboarding. A large camera sat on the table beside them.

I introduced myself. "I'm working on a documentary," I said knowing that "working on a documentary" should have been "a documentary is working on me." I was exhausted from this commitment, from the emotional drain and strain. Every day I wavered — *do it, don't do it, do it, don't*... That day was a *don't do it* day. I wanted to walk away, but I kept being pulled back. I wanted to tell the second half of the story — the story of Steve's killer. Not the story of a night or the story of a crime but the story of a *person*. Although I knew that as the general direction of the film, of the path, I was lost in repeated bouts of depression, kids who were falling apart that I couldn't help, people who didn't get me, and one change after the other in my educational, career, and personal goals.

But striking up a conversation in the coffee shop sealed the deal. Erik, the guy with the big camera, is now the film's director of photography. Once again, I had been placed in the perfect spot in the perfect moment. The path chose me, and pulled me back in — many days kicking and screaming.

So when someone asks *Where do I find God*? I respond, "He's in a coffee shop, of course."

First beach trip without Steve
Summer 2003

Acknowledgments

I am continually grateful for all of those people who believed in me, those people who wouldn't stop banging on my door until I dragged myself out of bed, those people who wouldn't stop calling when I pulled away: Lea and Joe, Johnny T, Angela and Phil, and Sara. For the "post Steve" friends I've come to love: John and Leigh, Don and Laurie, Eva, Deanna, Chris, Sarah, and Jill, and for my longtime friend (even on sabbatical) Angie. I am grateful to Debora for the constant tune-ups. Grateful to Sara for letting me write while drinking red wine on her white-carpeted floor; to the film crew — Erik, Ruth, Tamara, Amorette, and Christian — who believe in the raw and truthful telling of a story.

Thanks to Craig and Chris for getting this ball rolling. Thank you, Shana, for your willingness to be a part of my story and my brother's. Thanks to Aunt Lynn and Uncle Don and *all* of my Tennessee family for just that — family. Dr. Arrigo, Socratic teaching works! Thank you to the writers' group for encouraging me and for reading the roughest of drafts and seeing the diamond. Thanks to Tamara, my editor and my friend; you are the Hail Mary queen and without you this book would still be on scraps of paper and beverage napkins in the basket by my bed. Susan and Melissa, I so owe you margaritas!

I'm grateful to my entire family. Grief affects us all differently, and I get this. Thank you for respecting my path. Thank you to my parents, whose hearts and example made me...me. Thanks to my brother Joe who *has* found God, and my niece, Tami, and nephew, Matt.

Thank you to my children — Jessica, Trea, Tori, Jake, Caleb, and Gabby — for giving me a lot of second chances to be your mom. I'm grateful that *all* of you are part of my story and part of this story.

To my husband's family: for bringing groceries, gathering little kids, sorting through photos, and driving through snow so I'd see you in the back of the church — thank you.

I'm grateful to God for closing doors and opening

windows.

Mostly, I'm grateful to my husband, Doug, for understanding or ignoring or embracing every crazy piece of me.

Therese and Doug 2007